4 Steps to End Abortion

Chris Rush and Paul Lindquist

Table Of Contents

Introduction

For You formed my inward parts; You covered me in my mother's womb. I will praise You, for I am fearfully and wonderfully made; Marvelous are Your works, And that my soul knows very well. My frame was not hidden from You, When I was made in secret, And skillfully wrought in the lowest parts of the earth. Your eyes saw my substance, being yet unformed. And in Your book they all were written, The days fashioned for me, when as yet there were none of them. Psalm 139:13-16 (NKJV)

Abortion has been legal in America for well over a generation. And during that time, nearly 60 million babies have been slaughtered and deprived of their fundamental, God-given right to live. Clearly, something needs to change. We need a fresh vision and a new plan of action to put an end to this atrocity.

In this book, we lay out a simple, four-step plan that, once implemented, can end abortion in a surprisingly short period of time. Please read this with an open heart and consider what God is calling you to do personally to take up this fight.

Who We Are

We are #Allhandsondeck Media, a Christian not-for-profit organization that exists to see the end of legalized abortion in America. Our founders are Chris Rush and Paul Lindquist. Chris is an author, evangelist, speaker, founder of four ministries, and has a passion for working with the youth and protecting the unborn. Paul is an author, business writer, and owner of a copywriting service. He also has a passion for protecting the unborn.

I hope you can see, we are regular guys like anybody else. There is nothing special about us; and in our own strength, the idea of taking up the fight for the abolition of abortion is more than overwhelming. But we are not alone in this fight. God has put this on our hearts, and empowered us (through the humble guidance and direction of the Holy Spirit) to wake up the church to this issue and be used by God to see abortion end – for His glory.

The Birth of #Allhandsondeck

I became a Christian when I was 20. After becoming a believer, I became very active in ministry. During my 20s, I founded three ministries, did a lot of evangelizing, and really developed a heart for working with and mentoring youth.

I was meeting with a group of friends and we were praying for the youth in the inner-city. As we were praying, God began to bring up the issue of abortion in our hearts. One day while I was praying for the youth of the city, I felt the Lord speaking to me and saying "Chris, it's great what you're doing for the youth, but they're killing your youth before they even get to you."

During that time, as I was listening to talk radio during the Kermit Gosnell trials, I was hearing about the gruesome details of abortion, and my heart began to break. I was thinking, "is this real? Are we really talking about if it's legal to snip a baby's neck?"

Over time, as I fasted, prayed, and sought the Lord for this issue, using a red "Life" rubber band as a reminder to pray, I saw in my mind "#Allhandsondeck". I felt the Lord say that He was calling the whole church (e.g., pastors, janitors, children's workers, choir members...everybody) to address the issue of abortion head-on, the right way. And if done the right way, we could see abortion end in four years.

After hearing this, I began to go on a journey doing an inventory on the pro-life movement and the abortion abolitionist movement. In evaluating the current state of our movement, my conclusion was "something is totally wrong here. In the average year, over a million babies are aborted. If this were an NFL team or a major corporation and they were doing this poorly for this long, someone would end up getting fired, and something would definitely have to change."

Over time, looking at the good and the bad of the pro-life/abolitionist movement, I felt like the Lord gave me four simple steps on how we can see abortion end.

Chapter 1

Step One: Intense Prayer

Prayer is (or should be) the centerpiece of our Christian life. We have been taught to worship and pray daily; to thank God for our blessings, pray for our own needs, and intercede for the needs of others around us. Sadly, abortion has become such an accepted part of our culture that we don't pray against it like God would want us to.

We are calling on Christians to pray more intentionally and purposefully for the end of abortion. We believe prayer is paramount in this fight, and encourage it first and foremost. Here are the ways we believe you can pray most effectively:

- **Individual Prayer:** God is calling us as individuals to make praying for the end of abortion a daily routine (led by the Holy Spirit). As you pray personally for this issue, your own heart will begin to feel what God feels. We all have layers of apathy that can only be dealt with when we recognize we have a cold heart, and we bring it to God to set us on fire.

- **Family Intercession:** As we come together as a family to pray for the end of abortion, God begins to unite our households so we are of one mind and spirit on this issue. A family united praying against abortion has the power to shake a city.

- **Church Services:** We are encouraging every church to have a time set aside in their weekly service where they pray for the end of abortion. This does not have to be extremely long, but if the issue is brought up in services regularly, God will begin to give His heart to the larger congregation to begin to pick up the fight in whatever way He leads.

- **Prayer Meetings:** This is a great time for individuals to come together to focus intently on a topic and really labor for breakthrough in that area. As more and more prayer meetings begin to labor in prayer for the end of abortion, there is no doubt the end will quickly be seen. *And shall God not avenge His own elect who cry out day and night to Him, though He bears long with them. I tell you that He will avenge them speedily...* Luke 18:7-8 (NKJV).

- **Regional Gatherings:** Because abortion is a local, state, and national issue, we need the church to respond in kind. We need to have large gatherings where we come together as a corporate community and cry out to God for His mercy and intervention.

During these prayer times, take time to cry out to God for the lives of the unborn. Ask God to move the church away from apathy and into action on this issue. And prayerfully consider what God might be calling you to do to engage in this fight. Pray also for God to move the hearts of the pastors, church leaders, politicians and judiciary on this issue.

When we begin to pray intensely personally, as families, as churches, and even as cities, we will see some amazing things happen. God will begin to show you His heart for these precious souls, and you will begin to more clearly see the solution to this issue as God sees it.

Chapter 2

Step Two: Go to the Abortion Clinic

We believe going to the abortion clinic where they plan to commit murder day in and day out is a "love your neighbor" issue and not a special calling. The Bible says in Proverbs 24:11: "Deliver those who are drawn toward death, and hold back those stumbling to the slaughter" (NKJV).

In addition, if we really want to get the attention of our lawmakers, judiciary and the general public, we need to show up and *stand up* for the unborn souls who are being murdered day in and day out.

While at the clinic, there are a number of ways you can participate. For example, you can...

Pray

Most of us may say prayers here and there against abortion. But when you're at the clinic and praying, you get to see the faces of the girls who are walking into the clinic with the intention of killing their babies. This helps fuel a deeper sense of urgency in your prayers over this issue.

Hold a Sign

When you're at the clinic, there are several options for signs you can hold. My favorite is the sign that says "God loves you and your baby. Let us help you." Holding a sign outside the clinic sends a message to the girls going in, and to everyone who passes by.

I have seen many people change their minds from an abortion because what was being communicated with the sign struck their heart. This takes no special skills; just the commitment to show up and do it.

Talk to the Women and Men Going into the Abortion Clinics

This is clearly one of the most important activities during our time at the clinic. Speaking in a loving way, with urgency in your voice on behalf of the baby in the womb that has no voice, it can have a powerful effect on changing the mother's mind on having the abortion.

When you go to the abortion clinic and you speak to these girls, you are giving God the opportunity to speak directly to them through you. They get to hear the plea of the Father for that child's life, and the eternal life of the mother. I have seen countless women change their minds and keep their babies because of weak words I (and others) have spoken at the clinic.

When a girl pulls up at the abortion clinic, her ears are very much open. And though she may not seem like she's listening, your loving and truthful words are the last sensible words she's going to hear before she lays down on that abortion table.

Worship Jesus in Song and Create an Atmosphere of Worship There

Needless to say, when you worship Jesus in song as an individual, and definitely with a group, the atmosphere around you begins to change. You feel God's love and hear His voice.

The abortion clinic, from God's point of view, is a center for child sacrifice, an altar to Satan. When we gather outside of the abortion clinic and create an atmosphere of worship, God begins to dwell there in a tangible way.

We know that our God is light, and as we worship Him, the darkness that surrounds the clinic cannot stand against it. Worship can bring God into the waiting rooms of the abortion clinic, and from that place, hearts can be softened and babies can be saved.

Here's why showing up to the clinic is important. When we fail to show up, our absence speaks volumes about how important we really think this issue is.

Here's an example. One Saturday, I was the only one at the clinic. A man coming in to the clinic with a girl who had an appointment came up to me and said, "if this is so important, why are you the only one here?"

What do you say to that? I told him that unfortunately, the church is apathetic on this issue and they should be here. But still, no matter who shows up, murder is still murder, and every individual will be held accountable for his/her actions.

On the other hand, what would happen if we actually did show up? Let's take the Minneapolis/St Paul area as an example. There are over 3 million people living in the Twin Cities area, and over 50% of them claim to be Christian.

For this example, let's be super-conservative and assume there are only 100,000 Bible-believing Christians in the Twin Cities. If just 10% of them (10,000 people) showed up once a week at one of the four clinics in the area, you would have 2,500 Christians per week showing up at each clinic.

Think of the statement we could make if just 10% of the church in the Twin Cities decided to come out to the clinic and speak up for the unborn! When we start to show up with these types of numbers, several things will happen:

- It will be a sign to the girls walking in to have abortions that this issue truly matters;
- It will be a sign to the community, city and nation that the church is truly serious about putting an end to this atrocity;
- Our government leaders will take notice and realize that the church is

beginning to demand action on this issue.

Being at the clinic not only helps change the hearts of others, it changes your heart as well. My wife Autumn, after coming to the clinic, was emotionally moved and began crying over the babies that were being murdered inside. Autumn doesn't normally cry like that – I'm the crier in the family. But after spending some time in front of the clinic, her heart began to break over this issue.

By being at the clinic and seeing women going in to kill their babies in real time, abortion becomes more than just a "debating topic". By being right there on the ground, you will see first-hand who is going into the clinic.

One of the things you will learn very quickly (by being there) is that the girls who go in are not necessarily who you pictured in your mind. Most of us, when thinking about abortion in the abstract, picture girls going into the clinic who are young, poor, abandoned, and alone.

Some fit that description, but many earn above average income, drive nicer cars than you and I, are very prideful, and they are doing it for selfish reasons. Sadly, we also see quite a few girls with Christian bumper stickers on their cars going in to kill their babies.

When you show up at the clinic, it allows you to see this issue in a totally different light. Seeing the cars pull up and the women getting out to go into the clinic puts real faces to a real problem. Go out there once, and you'll see what I mean. After one day in front of that clinic, you won't be able look at abortion the same way again.

Chapter 3

Step Three: Getting LOUD in Our Culture

Our culture is a culture of death. We are apathetic, and with social media, we can stay distracted and avoid talking about complex, controversial issues.

We need to confront this issue head on, and there are many ways to do that in a way that brings attention to the need for the abolition of abortion. Here are some of them:

- Talk about abortion with family and friends (you must bring it up);
- Preach about the sin of abortion (after hearing in Christ) for those who need it;
- Go to the streets in your neighborhood to pass out abortion abolition literature, distribute drop cards, put posters on light poles, etc.;

- Help organize the movement through phone calls, e-mails, etc.;
- Raise funds for abolitionist projects, materials, staff and radio shows;
- Make yourself visible with the AHA (abolitionist) logo;
- Go to high schools to talk about abortion with students;
- Volunteer at the pregnancy help center;
- Start an abolitionist society in your high school, church or neighborhood;
- Attend weekly/monthly abolitionist meetings;
- Recruit people to local societies;
- Promote adoption and foster care;
- Give to #Allhandsondeck or any abolitionist society;
- Write letters to leaders, pastors, politicians sharing the need to abolish abortion;
- Facebook/blog about the topic;
- Make videos;
- Create plays focusing on abortion;
- Assemble newborn baskets stocked with diapers/wipes, clothes, formula, bottles, pacifiers, lotion, gift cards, etc.

When we pray and ask God to show us what He would have us do personally to end abortion, the creativity really begins to flow. Led by the Holy Spirit, saints across the land will start to put their energies into this issue.

The impact will be dynamic; and though it is impossible to predict exactly what will happen, one thing is for sure, the culture will hear us loud and clear on this issue. And they will know that we will not relent until this great evil is eradicated from our society.

Chapter 4

Step Four: DEMAND Abolition from our Leaders

For the last 44 years, we have seen 100s of different tactics to try to deal with the issue of abortion. And if we are just being honest with ourselves, they all have failed.

In the days of Moses, after a few devastating judgments on Egypt, the Pharaoh tried to strike up a deal with Moses to let some of the people go. In response, Moses essentially said there are no negotiations with the King of Heaven, "LET MY PEOPLE GO!!"

Though the heart and the intentions of many people who have attempted to limit abortions and regulate the industry to a place where more babies can be saved are honorable, this approach is deeply flawed. When it comes to innocent human life, we do not negotiate with murderers and with Satan!

It is time that we begin to just simply demand what we all want – the complete abolition of abortion. We must demand from our government leaders at all levels to work tirelessly for the end of abortion.
Politicians are known for paying lip service to various causes, especially to the pro-life lobby. They are professionals at making you feel like they truly care. Though some may, they will only truly do something when they fear that their jobs hinge on making good on their promises to end abortion.

A lot of people want politicians to put their careers on the line and their necks on the chopping block for the issue of abortion, but these same people are unwilling to do everything ***they*** can to abolish abortion. This is why demanding abolition from our politicians is Step Four in the process.

When we show, through our own personal sacrifices of time, energy and reputation, that we are committed to the cause of abortion abolition, this will either inspire politicians to finally do what is right, or it will expose those who are truly paying lip service to our movement.

A day is coming (and yet with the start of this campaign it is already here) where if you are not a politician who is for the total abolition of abortion, you will be removed from your position. No matter how much you smile and say we are making progress with baby steps, that strategy will no longer be acceptable to the church that is *burning* for this issue.

Here's an example of what we mean. If it takes Texas 40 years to simply enact a 20-week ban on abortion, how long are we estimating it will take Texas to enact a 12-week ban? And how long, from there, are we estimating it will take for total abolition?

If this is the strategy for advancing the abolition of abortion in arguably the most conservative state in the Union, then how long will it take the rest of us to get rid of this great evil? 100 years? 150 years? Why not just ask for what we want – "**ABOLISH ABORTION NOW**"!!

If we are consistent with the first three steps, then this last step will very easily fall into place. How long does that mean it will take to end abortion? No one can know for sure, but we believe it can be ended within the next four years. If we keep repeating the same demand and stay united, no wall of lies, deceit and manipulation can withstand this all-powerful wrecking ball.

If you are a politician and you're reading this book, you need to understand that God is the one who grants authority to all government leaders. He gives authority and power for the purposes of establishing righteousness and justice.

At this very moment, the souls that have been aborted are crying out for justice. Are you hearing them?

Many people in politics live by the saying "it's the economy, stupid". When legalized murder is going on under your authority, believe me, from the Lord's perspective, the last thing He wants to talk about is the economy.

When you stand before God on the day of judgment, you will be held accountable for the things you did and didn't do with the power He gave you. Do you really think He will be impressed with the fact that you lowered taxes or designed a better health care plan?

He is longing that the people He has given authority to will pick up His heart and fight for what He deems worthy in this hour. Be one the Lord can smile at on that Day and say "well done, good and faithful servant." Mr.

and Mrs. Politician, don't squander this opportunity to use the authority you've been given to defend the weakest among us. Fight for the end of abortion!

Chapter 5:

Turning the Hearts of the Fathers to the Children

For behold, the day is coming, Burning like an oven, And all the proud, yes, all who do wickedly will be stubble. And the day which is coming shall burn them up, Says the Lord of hosts, That will leave them neither root nor branch.

But to you who fear My name The Sun of Righteousness shall arise With healing in His wings; And you shall go out And grow fat like stall-fed calves.

You shall trample the wicked, For they shall be ashes under the soles of your feet On the day that I do this, Says the Lord of hosts.

Remember the Law of Moses, My servant, Which I commanded him in Horeb for all Israel, With the statutes and judgments.

Behold, I will send you Elijah the prophet Before the coming of the great and dreadful day of the Lord.

And he will turn The hearts of the fathers to the children, And the hearts of the children to their fathers, Lest I come and strike the earth with a curse.

Malachi 4 (NKJV)

This End Times chapter is very significant. It shows the heart of God. God is a Father with a huge heart for His children. So much so, He says, that when He looks upon the earth, if He does not see His heart reflected in the sons of men, there will be a curse on the land.

God wants men to begin to be like their Father in Heaven, and turn their sights to children who they cannot profit from (and cannot be paid back from), and give their whole lives to see them fulfill their destiny.

Men turning to acknowledge the issue of abortion and adopting an unrelenting commitment to fight it is fulfilling Malachi 4:6. This will bring a blessing to the earth by glorifying the Father in Heaven, who is unrelenting and committed in the fight for our souls.

It is time, men, to rise up and turn our hearts to the weakest among us. And by doing so, their hearts will be turned us.

The danger is, if we do NOT turn our hearts to the babies in the womb, God is promising to strike our land, and take everything from us that we hold dear. We've been given an open door at this time in our history to end abortion. We must seize this moment, while it is here, because soon, the door will close.

So in other words, if we allow abortion to continue, we cannot expect God to continue to bless ourselves, our homes, and our land. But we **can** expect to be on the receiving end of God's judgment, like an axe to a tree. So be wise, men, and love God's inheritance like it was your own.

Chapter 6:

Be a Horton and be a "Who"

After I felt the Lord speaking to me #Allhandsondeck, He eventually led me to a movie called *Horton Hears a Who* (by Dr. Seuss). The main point of the movie is Horton is an elephant in the jungle who finds a speck that has life in it. He ends up communicating with the leader of the village of "Whos" that live on this speck, but they do not know they are on a speck.

From Horton's perspective, he's communicating to a little ball of dust. From the mayor's perspective, he's speaking to the invisible elephant in the sky. The movie is about the characters in Horton's jungle who want to take the speck Horton is talking to and destroy it, because they think he is crazy.

The whole movie, Horton is protecting the speck and his motto is "a person is a person, no matter how small." From the perspective of the mayor, he is trying to get all of Whoville to join him in raising up their voices so that the characters in Horton's jungle can hear them.

In the climax of the movie, the mayor gets every "Who" to say "we are here!!" Some do it by playing instruments, some by singing, most by just outright yelling it. Whoville gets saved when the last "Who" (who is a youth) adds his voice and says "yopp!!" At that point, the characters in Horton's jungle can hear sound coming from the speck, and Whoville is saved.

God has used this movie to show us how we should fight abortion. For one, we have to be like Horton, who protects life no matter the cost or the size of the life. We must be a people who says "a person is a person, no matter how small."

We also have to be like the "Whos" in Whoville, who in unity, came together, and said "we are here!!" And just like in the movie, the youngest among us will rise up with their small voices and be the straw that finally breaks the dragon's back.

So we must together say in unity "ABOLISH ABORTION NOW!!" Just like in Whoville, the fight wasn't over until every "Who" spoke up. In the same manner, this fight is not over until every Christian speaks up (using their own unique gifts and talents) and we reach the tipping point when our government leaders finally hear us shouting on behalf of the pre-born children.

Chapter 7:

#Allhandsondeck is a Campaign

#Allhandsondeck has a fresh and unique approach to fighting for the end of abortion. We are a campaign in the sense that we want to help lead this movement to the finish line. Though we want individuals and churches to be led by the Spirit to come up with creative ways to advance the cause, we want to be a well-funded organization that is helping to guide and direct these efforts in a tangible way.

For example, we want to help churches cultivate prayer in their services and plan city-wide prayer gatherings to cry out to God for the end of abortion. We want to be a campaign that helps gather pastors and leaders to fight as one body for abolition. We also want to plan marches and big concerts with big names to bring awareness to the issue.

In addition, we want to plan local and national tours to spread this message throughout the land. We want to be an organization that sponsors a unique billboard campaign across the nation. We want to run commercials and even run a Super Bowl commercial so we can announce to the whole nation that the end of abortion is near.

We want to be a campaign with staff who are called to spread the message of abolition full-time in their local communities. We want to be a campaign that national leaders (including the President of the United States) are hearing loud and clear and do more than just give us a seat at the table, but take our lead to take aggressive action to see our nation washed clean from the sin of abortion.

We need every hand in this fight, so we are asking that you partner with us in whatever way the Lord is leading to help spearhead this movement. Please contact us; your prayers, your financial support, your volunteering, your platform, and your talents are needed for the success of #Allhandsondeck. When we join together, we will have victory.

Chapter 8:

End Abortion: Send Revival

Years ago, I went to a conference and there was a man there by the name of Lou Engle whom God had gripped for the unborn and the end of abortion. God had led him to come up with a prayer that soon was spoken by millions across the nation. The prayer was "God, I plead your blood over my sins and the sins of this nation. End abortion, and send revival to America."

For decades, Christians in America have been crying out for revival. When we see our nation and the moral corruption around us, the lack of worship in the hearts of people, the promotion of ungodliness, and the purposelessness of our youth, it makes the people of God fall on their faces and cry out for a move of the Holy Spirit like in the days old. God has promised an End Time harvest of billions of souls. Many people are going to come to the Lord before the return of Jesus. The time is near, and the Lord is ready to show His glory to the earth. Our job is to prepare for it.

The Bible says that children are an inheritance unto the Lord. We believe before we see revival in our land, we **must** see God's inheritance protected. Just like Moses was protected from Pharaoh's rage, and kept hidden when they were murdering all the Israelite babies in Egypt for him to later lead the people out of slavery and into the promised land, we must end abortion so we can enter into the promised land of revival.

We are supposed to be a people preparing the way for the Lord's return. And what if ending abortion is doing just that? Yes, there are many injustices in the land, such as poverty and sex trafficking just to name a couple, but abortion stands above them all.

In the story of David and Goliath, if we are Davids standing against an army that wants to destroy us, there is one giant in our enemy's army that is more fierce than the others, and that is the legalized murder of 3000 pre-born children in America *every day* (aka abortion). But just like David and the Israelites, when we take out the giant of abortion, the other injustices will quickly flee like the Philistine army did.

We have to stop trusting in our government leaders to really care enough to do what it takes to end abortion. We've been doing that for well over 40 years. Even one of our greatest presidents, Ronald Reagan, let us down on this issue by appointing two Supreme Court justices (Sandra Day O'Connor and Anthony Kennedy) who were not committed to administering justice for the unborn.

We have to stop believing the abortion lobby and their allies in the Democrat Party are the reason that abortion remains legal. The true cause is the church's lack of crying out for justice for the unborn, and a lack of willingness to get their own hands dirty and demand the abolition of abortion from our leaders.

We have to stop being distracted by hollow victories like abortion restrictions and defunding Planned Parenthood. This should not be the goal. Every life is precious in God's eyes, and only the total abolition of abortion protects the lives of God's entire inheritance.

Chapter 9:

End Game

There are several ways abortion could be abolished. Here are some possible scenarios:

- State governments abolishing abortion in their states;
- State governors declaring "sanctuary states" for the pre-born where abortion is longer allowed;
- A new *Convention of States* being called to amend the Constitution to abolish abortion;
- A "personhood" case before the Supreme Court that rightly compels the court to find abortion unconstitutional;
- An amendment to the U.S. Constitution (passed by 2/3 of Congress and ¾ of the states) that abolishes abortion.

We do not know exactly how abortion will be abolished in America. With an on-fire church willing to do what God tells them to do, the possibilities are limitless.

When the church rises up with the 4 steps and they are praying with an unceasing cry, going to the clinics in mass numbers, getting loud in countless creative ways, and all demanding the same thing -- END ABORTION NOW!! -- we will storm the culture with such overwhelming force that it will be impossible for abortion to remain legal.

We must first recognize that we must change the way we are fighting. In the book of Revelation, Jesus says to the church of Laodicea:

Because you say, 'I am rich, have become wealthy, and have need of nothing'—and do not know that you are wretched, miserable, poor, blind, and naked. I counsel you to buy from Me gold refined in the fire, that you may be rich; and white garments, that you may be clothed, that the shame of your nakedness may not be revealed; and anoint your eyes with eye salve, that you may see. Revelation 3:17-18 (NKJV).

It is time for the church to hear this call of #Allhandsondeck and buy into what we have written in this book as if it was refined gold. Agree to carry out these steps so we may become rich with God's inheritance, which is the pre-born (that would have been aborted) walking the earth and carrying out God's purposes for their lives.

#Allhandsondeck is a campaign to end abortion within the next four years. We are in need of your partnership and financial support for us to be successful. Please visit our website at allhandsondeckmedia.com and contact us to let us know how we can partner together to see our goal achieved.

We want to connect with pastors, leaders, media personalities, musicians, youth groups, business owners, politicians, and anyone else who has a heart for our cause to help amplify the message of #Allhandsondeck. This is the hour, and for such a time as this, **you** have now been called to be part of the most important campaign since the end of slavery. Welcome aboard!!

Contact Information

To join our movement or receive further information about our campaign, please visit:

www.allhandsondeckmedia.com

To partner financially with us, go to:

https://www.allhandsondeckmedia.com/contribute/

You may also contact us in one of the following ways:

Email:
allhandsondeckmediamn@gmail.com

Facebook:
https://www.facebook.com/christopher.rush.104

By Phone Toll Free at: 1-800-933-7681

Made in the USA
Monee, IL
01 March 2021

60502940R00024